I0572652

# On The Job
# in the Game

by Jessica Cohn

RED
CHAIR
•PRESS•

Please visit our website at **www.redchairpress.com** for more high-quality products for young readers.

**Publisher's Cataloging-In-Publication Data**

Cohn, Jessica.
  On the job in the game / by Jessica Cohn.

  pages : illustrations ; cm. -- (On the job)

  Summary: "Coaches, referees. Some jobs in sports are easy to name because we see them on the field of play. But who makes sure we stay safe when we play? Let's take a look at all the important players beyond the field by going On the Job in the Game."--Provided by publisher.

  Includes writing activity and first-person interview.
  Includes bibliographical references and index.
  ISBN: 978-1-63440-111-1 (library hardcover)
  ISBN: 978-1-63440-117-3 (paperback)
  ISBN: 978-1-937529-55-0 (ebook)

  1. Sports--Vocational guidance--Juvenile literature. 2. Sports--Vocational guidance. I. Title. II. Title: In the game

GV705.4 .C64 2016
796.023                                                            2015953628

**Illustration credits:** p. 4, 9, 10, 13, 14, 16, 17 (top, bottom), 18, 20, 21, 28 (top, bottom), 30: Lauren Scheuer

**Photo credits:** Cover, p. 1, 3, 4, 5 (top), 7 (all), 8, 9, 10-11, 12, 13, 14, 15 (bottom left, bottom right), 16, 17, 19, 20-21, 24 (left, right), 25 (left, right), 26, 27 (bottom): Shutterstock; p. 5 (bottom): British Library; p. 6, 27: Dreamstime; p. 18, 28-29: iStock; p. 22, 23: Lauren Ramirez; p. 32: Nathan Cohn

This series first published by:
Red Chair Press LLC          PO Box 333          South Egremont, MA 01258-0333

Printed in the United States of America

Distributed in the U.S. by Lerner Publisher Services.  www.lernerbooks.com

0516  1  WRZF16

# Table of Contents

# Jobs in the Field

*The players line up on the court. They listen to "The Star-Spangled Banner." The song ends, and the crowd roars. It's game time!*

What would life be like without sports? It's hard to think of it. Each day, people work in gyms with goals in mind. Teams meet on courts and fields. "Team sports will be in my life for as long as I live," says Jesse Cohen of California.

Playing makes people stronger both in mind and body. The games people play teach sportsmanship. That means playing fairly. It is treating others well, whether as winners or losers.

## The Long Game

**2000 B.C.** The ancient Chinese build structures to hold sporting events.

**776 B.C.** The ancient Greeks hold the first Olympic Games.

**A.D. 1100** Native Americans play lacrosse as an organized sport.

**18th Century** The colonists in America play organized games of cricket.

# In the Game

Most people play sports to exercise. The activities help grow skills like aim and balance. Plus, it's fun to shoot hoops. It feels good to run. But sports can also be highly organized. The games need planning. The players need help. So an interest in sports can lead to work that relates. Big events bring in thousands of fans. Countless jobs are tied to them.

# Winning Ways

Surfing, anyone? Snowboarding? People play to win in all kinds of events. Race fans cheer on their favorite drivers. Soccer matches bring in large crowds dressed in team colors. Each sport has events—and this field of careers seems to keep growing.

Not long ago, new **leagues** formed for **disc sports**. These sports have been around a while, but more people want to see them played by teams on big fields. So Cohen can now play Ultimate as a **professional**. That's a disc game with end zones. "I cherish the . . . trust and responsibility required in a team sport such as Ultimate," he says.

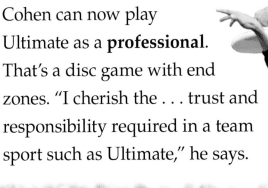

# Playing Along

Pro sports are not the only games in town. Plenty of work involves helping **amateurs**. They practice in schools, clubs, and other places that are set up for workouts.

Some of these athletes work like pros. For example, thousands of young people are in training for the Olympics now. They want to win medals for their countries. They put in long hours to try to win a spot on a team. The Olympic Games take place every four years. These athletes want to be ready for the next events.

### What are the biggest U.S. pro leagues?

The four biggest leagues for U.S. professionals are the MLB, the NBA, the NFL, and the NHL. These stand for Major League Baseball, the National Basketball Association, the National Football League, and the National Hockey League.

## Going to College

Workers can also get in the game at the college level. Football starts up each fall. Basketball happens in winter. Big colleges have programs that they run like businesses. The players are the best in their fields. Their fans are willing to travel a long way to cheer them on.

The schools also have **intramural** sports. The players compete with others within the school. Or they play other teams in the area. These programs need workers, too.

# Fields of Glory

The players get the glory. But the fans also value the people who run things. For example, Tommy Lasorda was a baseball player. He was not a star. Then, he gave up playing and became a manager. Now, people remember him well for his winning teams.

"In baseball and in business, there are three types of people," he once said. What are they? They are "those who make it happen, those who watch it happen, and those who wonder what happened."

**What is the work of an agent like?**

Agents guide athletes. They help players find places to play. They try to get their **clients** the best deals.

The day may start and end with research. The agent has to know what is going on in the business. STEM studies are important. Agents need math skills. They need to know law related to **contracts**. They must communicate well.

*Tommy Lasorda*

# The Front Office

**B**usiness skills can lead to jobs in the "front office." In the pros, those are high-powered positions. The managers in pro sports have to make hard decisions. They choose players, and they let them go. It's their job to gain a winning edge.

The programs need assistants, too. "Some of my projects include finding all of the stories written about the team each day," says Stuart Dezenhall. He works for a football team in New York. He helps players and coaches get ready for interviews. He supports "the team's efforts both on and off the field."

# A Day's Work

Dezenhall followed his interest in sports to get to where he is. "My favorite part of my career is being around a professional sports team," he says. "[A] lot of the work that I do seems more like fun than it does like work."

# Path for a Manager

Want to work in the world of sports? Do you understand the needs of business? Saying yes to these questions is the first step to working in **administration** or becoming a manager.

>> **You Know It!**

The money made at sports structures is more than $300 billion each year. That makes it one of the largest industries in North America.

## Getting the Job

### Skills
Need leadership, sports knowledge, and STEM skills (for deals and decisions)

### Duties
Manage a player, a team, or an entire sport. Plan programs. Follow trends related to the sport and the fans. Represent your groups. Find and manage **funding**.

### Education
1. Get **bachelor's degree**.

2. Make contacts in the industry, such as through **internships**.

3. May start in sales, such as ticket sales.

4. May also want to earn a law degree or a **master's degree** in business.

# Working It

The people in the office need to understand **promotion**. They must do what they can to make their team or sport popular. Selling tickets is what keeps them in business. Their teams are like **brands**.

Some of the workers do **merchandising**. They make and sell T-shirts and other products. They raise money to help their programs and players succeed. But getting work in a front office is harder now than ever. Many people want these jobs. A person must be ready to compete to get one.

# First Jobs

Can you see yourself working in a front office? Many people start as assistants, or they work for teams in lower leagues that feed the higher ones. They take classes in sports management to get a foot in the door. Some of the related jobs include:

- Sales
- **Facility** worker
- Marketing assistant
- Communications assistant

**Are there other ways to break into this field?**
College students can mix their interest in sports with travel. Some groups match students with work as coaches in other countries. The students must learn to manage their players. The challenge is also to learn about people in another land and to grow from it.

# Taking the Field

*"Rock-climbing teachers help their students to be 'boulder.'"*

You do not have to help pros to be a pro. Towns across the country look for help to build up their sports programs. Parks need people to run their leagues. **Recreation** groups hire teachers. Fitness groups need leaders.

Their buildings and grounds have to be kept in shape. Otherwise these important programs cannot take place. It is a big job keeping these areas ready for play.

Around the world, parks and community centers hire fitness instructors.

# Great Outdoors

A special interest in outdoor sports can turn into a related line of work. Sports stores have classes for skills such as boating. Businesses offer equipment and classes for sports like windsurfing. Health clubs teach rock climbing. These organizations all need people to run things.

# Counting on It

*"We use stats to predict how valuable a player will be in the future. . . ."*
—Ben Lowry from the Oakland A's

Good with numbers? Sports can also be a numbers game. Teams need workers who collect **data** on the plays and players. People get paid to study the numbers.

"[A] lot of what we try to determine is how much of a player's success we should attribute to skill versus luck, " says Ben Lowry. A stat (statistic) is a fact such as how likely it is that a player will hit the ball. To do his work in baseball he looks at stats from many seasons. This is because "over a short period . . . a stat . . . can [change] purely based on chance."

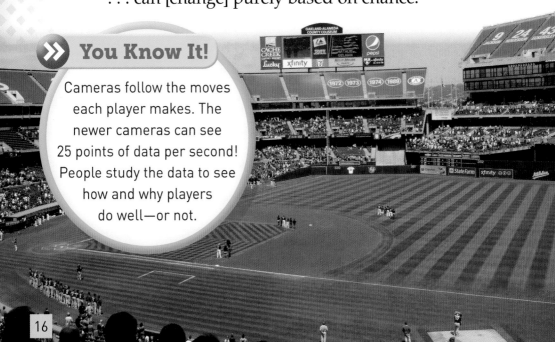

## >> You Know It!

Cameras follow the moves each player makes. The newer cameras can see 25 points of data per second! People study the data to see how and why players do well—or not.

# In That Number

Numbers can show new ways to win. Baseball's Oakland A's were losing. Then, they started looking at what players could do instead of what players could not do. They stopped paying for a few players who did a lot of things well. Instead, they paid to have more players. The managers studied what each person could deliver. They did the best they could with those facts. The team started to win.

The ability to work with numbers can also lead to jobs in finance. That's the management of money. Sports programs also need finance people with STEM skills.

## What is a consultant?

**Statisticians** often work as consultants. This means they get hired to come in and give advice. They collect data. Then, they make sure the data is worthwhile. They study the facts to find strengths in the teams.

# Player Health

*"Every week, an NFL team loses two to ten players to injury."*
—*Dr. David Geier, on his blog about sports medicine*

Keeping players healthy is a field of its own. It appeals to people with interests in both sports and medicine. For example, pro teams need to have their own doctors. A doctor shows up before a game to see how the players are doing. He or she stands by while they play in case someone gets hurt. A whistle blows. The doctor runs!

These workers prepare and protect the players. A doctor for a hockey team said that he sees each game as "three thousand six hundred seconds" of danger. Sometimes he can watch and just enjoy it. Other times, he is called in.

# What's Up, Doc?

Doctors go to college for eight to ten years. Sports doctors get extra training. They need to understand what happens when the body moves.

The doctors assist when players get hurt. They test players for harmful drugs. They give helpful exercises to players. A team doctor teaches the whole team about important matters of health.

 **You Know It!**

**Acute injuries** are sudden. For example, a player may suddenly not be able to put weight on a foot. A **chronic injury** happens after playing a long time. For example, a player may feel dull pain while moving a shoulder.

## Joint Efforts

Many people who are injured in sports have problems with their joints in later years. Up to half of them do. Doctors and athletic trainers can show people how to move in ways that help them avoid tears in their muscles.

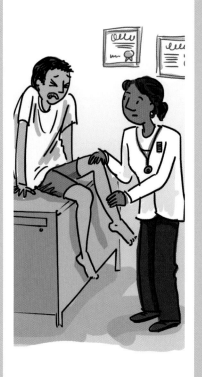

# In Training

*1-2-3. Breathe. Stretch. Strengthen.* Even athletes need to be shown how to care for their muscles. So athletic trainers teach ways to warm up and stretch. These workers can also give first aid if it's needed. They can help players heal when they are hurt.

Most athletic trainers have master's degrees. Some have even more education. They work in hospitals, in schools, and for teams. They also help other kinds of performers, such as dancers.

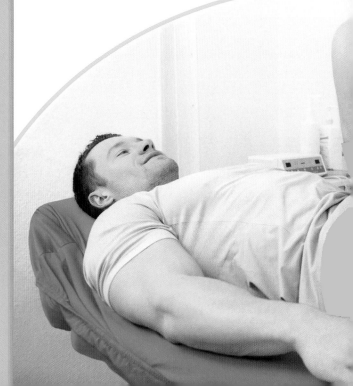

# Degree of Health

Those with interest in this field can study sports medicine. They can learn about kinesiology. That is the science of body movements. Its students learn about the parts of the body and how the parts work together. People with this know-how can show coaches how to help their players practice. A set of exercises can make a difference. It can mean that fewer people end up hurt.

**What is adaptive recreation?**

Workers who know sports medicine can also help people with special challenges. They can work with people who are missing limbs or are in wheel chairs. Becoming a health-care giver in this field requires STEM skills.

**Jamie K. Woodall**, LAT, ATC, is the head athletic trainer at James Earl Rudder High School in Bryan, Texas.

**1 What do you like best about the work?**

My favorite part of athletic training is watching an athlete come back from an injury and be successful in his or her sport. I also enjoy educating athletes on how to be healthier and perform better.

**2 What experience and education led you to this?**

I have always liked participating in sports and also wanted a career in health care. Athletic training allows me to be in the sports environment as well as to help others who are injured or ill.

I continue to be active as a runner and participate in races. When I become injured, I know how to treat my own injuries and can prevent them from happening in the future.

**3** **What advice would you give to a student who is interested in this line of work?**

Although I work in a high school, many athletic trainers work in other settings, such as professional sports, industry, and hospitals. Regardless of the setting, athletic training is a high-energy profession with a focus on science. Students who are interested in a career in athletic training should learn about the human body and how it works.

# Supporting Roles in Sports

**E**vents need guards. Teams have drivers. Think about everything it must take to put on a big or even a small event in sports. Many workers play a part in the sports world. They help players, teams, and fans in different ways.

## Lawyer

Players, coaches, and others call on lawyers. Lawyers help team owners write up deals. They write contracts for players and coaches. Sometimes, they step in to help when someone has been hurt. They may help a player get the support needed to heal.

## Facility Designer

The buildings where teams play hold large crowds. Some people mix sports with a desire to build these structures. They study the special needs of large gathering places, such as the size of emergency exits. Then they can plan and build these huge spaces.

## Event Manager

Event managers make events happen. They work to make sure that big games and other events are safe, fun, and successful. In the large structures that hold sporting events, it's a big job. The people need to be able to handle many details. These managers must be able to work with many kinds of workers.

## Food and Beverage Manager

It's also a big job to feed visitors at stadiums. Who plans what to serve? How do they get that much food ready? Managers in this field are highly organized, good with numbers, and able to work well with others. They need to handle stocks of food as well as manage big budgets.

# Hey, Coach!

To stay in the game, close to the players, some people become coaches. Pro teams have a team of coaches. They teach skills and give pep talks. Coaches need to know their sport inside and out to be able to help athletes be the best they can be.

Coaches also help single players, schools, and other groups. They need to know some first aid to be ready to act in case of an injury. For this and other reasons, coaches often need special certificates from the states where they work. They get degrees in fitness.

## Scout It Out

Teams are always on the lookout for new players. Some people make it their job to find this new talent. They act as scouts. They work for teams or they act as part of a group that gives advice to teams.

Scouts must know their sports well, so they are often former players. They travel the country, looking for people. Scouts decide how much effort it will take to get new players up to speed. They suggest ways that teams can use and help people.

**How do you become a game official?**
Game officials have to stay calm and make quick decisions. They need a sense of fairness. Most of them start by joining the local group of officials in the sport that they wish to judge. They learn from long-time judges how to call plays on their own.

## The SID

The SID is the sports information director. At a college, a SID often has to track facts for one or more sports. He or she may work on the website or talk to people in the media.

# For Your Information

Skill with words can be a ticket to a job as well. There are jobs "inside" sports for writers and speakers. They send out info about their teams, games, and players.

Is there a game on? It's never too early to start to study how to do this job. "I got involved in sports communications because of my love of sports," says Stuart Dezenhall. He is working his way up in football. "I grew up playing and watching sports," he says. He "always loved listening to what players and coaches said and reading stories about the team."

Reporters cover events from the outside. They tell stories and share facts and video. Others talk about the events while they are happening. They announce scores and plays.

# At Work in Sports

**E**vent Manager. Coach. Athletic Trainer. General Manager. Player. Sports Information Director. Team Doctor.

It may be that you just want to keep your eyes on the game when it is happening, but it takes many workers to make events like that happen. Teams and the places they play are run like businesses, and they have jobs for people with all kinds of skills.

Are you interested in sports and fitness?

Do you see yourself making a difference in one of the many roles in sports?

Can you learn to do the work by putting in time and taking classes?

Perhaps you will one day work on the job in sports.

# Extension
## Sports Report!

Think about the sport that interests you the most. Is there a game or a meet that you can watch and report on?

### Before

Look for sports reports to study what you will need to know. Your readers need to know who is playing. They need to know what happens and where and when. They need to know why one player or team wins.

### During

Be present for the entire event. Watch carefully. Take notes. Look for a program with the names of the players. You can use that or a related website to check your spelling.

### After

Tell the story. What happened in what order? What was the outcome? Is there one athlete you can focus on? Perhaps you can get that person to comment on what happened.

Make sure to cover basic facts. Take time to check your facts. Take time to punch up the language, too. Sports writers can often have fun with words. You can, too!

# Glossary

acute injuries  harm and pain experienced in the first days after the body is hurt

administration  process of running an organization; those who do this work

amateurs  those who participate without expecting to be paid

bachelor's degree  earned for three to five years of study after high school

brands  names or related features that make one product, person, or group special

chronic injury  harm and pain that develops over time and is felt regularly

clients  people or groups that hire someone's services

contracts  written agreements that explain what will be done and not done by whom

data  facts and figures

disc sports  games played with flat, round objects rather than balls

facility  place and equipment used for events such as games of sport

funding  money or similar resource needed to pay for something

internships  on-the-job training, usually without pay

intramural  happening within a place or a certain community

leagues  collections of groups that meet for a purpose, such as competing in games

master's degree  earned for mastery of subject at least one year beyond bachelor's degree

merchandising  selling items or a brand to people, using a careful plan and timing

professional  having to do with a career for pay in a certain field or profession

promotion  activity that draws attention or encourages support

recreation  an enjoyable activity done when not working

statisticians  those who are experts collecting and understanding facts and numbers

# Index

## >> Meet the Author

**Jessica Cohn** has made a career of writing and editing materials for young people, covering varied topics, from social studies and science to poetry. If you ask her, Cohn will tell you that she feels lucky to be on the job in educational publishing. Each day, she discovers something new to learn and someone with an interesting story—and then gets to share the information. Jessica and her family reside in California. When not working, she enjoys hiking, helping her local library, and exploring the country.